BREAKFAST
Across Cultures
Recipes from Around the World

by
Chelsey Luciow

CAPSTONE PRESS
a capstone imprint

Dabble Lab is published by Capstone Press, an imprint of Capstone.
1710 Roe Crest Drive, North Mankato, Minnesota 56003
capstonepub.com

Copyright © 2025 by Capstone. All rights reserved. No part of this publication may be reproduced in whole or in part, or stored in a retrieval system, or transmitted in any form or by any means, electronic, mechanical, photocopying, recording, or otherwise, without written permission of the publisher.

Library of Congress Cataloging-in-Publication Data is available on the Library of Congress website.
ISBN: 9781669093015 (hardcover)
ISBN: 9781669092971 (ebook PDF)

Summary: Get a taste of the world when you cook up breakfast across cultures! From French crepes to Jamaican steamed cabbage to Chinese zucchini pancakes, these easy-to-make recipes are sure to help you start the day off right.

Image Credits: Adobe Stock: Obsessively (background), 18, 29, Sharmin, 13 (background);
Mighty Media, Inc. (project photos)
Design Elements: Adobe Stock: byMechul, zhaluldesign; Mighty Media, Inc.

Editorial Credits
Editor: Jessica Rusick
Designer: Denise Hamernik

Any additional websites and resources referenced in this book are not maintained, authorized, or sponsored by Capstone. All product and company names are trademarks™ or registered® trademarks of their respective holders.

The publisher and the author shall not be liable for any damages allegedly arising from the information in this book, and they specifically disclaim any liability from the use or application of any of the contents of this book.

Printed and bound in China. 6096

Table of Contents

Cooking Up Breakfast 4

French Crepes 6

German Strammer Max 8

Mexican Chilaquiles Verdes 11

Spanish Magdalenas 12

Jamaican Steamed Cabbage 15

Zimbabwean Cornmeal Porridge 16

Irish Full Breakfast 19

Moroccan Avocado Almond Smoothie Bowl 20

Chinese Zucchini Pancakes 23

Hawaiian Banana Bread 24

Belarusian Draniki Potato Pancakes 27

Indian Rava Uttapam 28

Venezuelan Arepas 31

    Read More 32

    Internet Sites 32

    About the Author 32

Cooking Up
BREAKFAST

Breakfast is the first meal of the day and maybe the most important! Kids in countries around the world eat all kinds of breakfast food before starting their days. Many meals are beloved dishes in the cultures they come from. Make a Moroccan smoothie bowl, a full Irish breakfast, Mexican chilaquiles, and more to experience foods from across cultures!

Basic Supplies

- baking sheet
- blender
- cupcake tin
- frying pan
- grater
- knife and cutting board
- measuring cups and spoons
- mixing bowls
- parchment paper
- spatula

Kitchen Tips

1. Ask an adult for permission before you make a recipe.

2. Ask an adult for help when using a knife, blender, grater, stove, or oven. Wear oven mitts when removing items from the oven or microwave.

3. Read through the recipe and set out all ingredients and supplies before you start working.

4. Using metric tools? Use the conversion chart on the right to make your recipe measure up.

5. Wash your hands before and after you handle food. Wash and dry fresh produce before use.

6. When you are done making food, clean your work surface and wash dirty dishes. Put all supplies and ingredients back where you found them.

Standard	Metric
¼ teaspoon	1.25 grams or milliliters
½ teaspoon	2.5 g or mL
1 teaspoon	5 g or mL
1 tablespoon	15 g or mL
¼ cup	57 g (dry) or 60 mL (liquid)
⅓ cup	75 g (dry) or 80 mL (liquid)
½ cup	114 g (dry) or 125 mL (liquid)
⅔ cup	150 g (dry) or 160 mL (liquid)
¾ cup	170 g (dry) or 175 mL (liquid)
1 cup	227 g (dry) or 240 mL (liquid)
1 quart	950 mL

French Crepes

Crepes are a French handheld street food dating back hundreds of years. They are rolled or folded and can have sweet or savory fillings and toppings.

Ingredients
(makes 6 to 8 crepes)

- 2 cups all-purpose flour
- ¼ teaspoon salt
- 2 large eggs
- 2 cups milk
- shortening
- 8 ounces whipped topping
- maple syrup (optional)
- fresh berries (optional)
- powdered sugar (optional)

1. Combine the flour and salt in a large mixing bowl. Whisk in the eggs and milk to make the batter.

2. Put 2 tablespoons of shortening in a frying pan over medium heat. Let the shortening melt.

3. Pour some batter into the middle of the pan. Tilt the pan in all directions to spread the batter out.

4. Cook the crepe for about 2 minutes on one side. The edges should be crispy and the middle should have bubbles. Flip the crepe with a spatula and cook it for another 2 minutes. Then use the spatula to slide the crepe onto the plate.

5. Repeat steps 3 and 4 to make more crepes. Add more shortening if the pan looks dry.

6. Spoon a line of whipped topping down the center of each crepe. Then roll the crepes up. If you'd like, serve your crepes with maple syrup, fresh berries, and powdered sugar.

Little Lunch

The French word for "breakfast" is *petit-déjeuner* (PUH-tee DAY-zhuh-nay), which means "little lunch."

German Strammer Max

This open-faced sandwich became popular in Germany after World War II. The dish is beloved because it is simple to make and features common ingredients.

Ingredients
(makes 2 sandwiches)

- butter
- 2 slices of rye bread
- 4 slices of cured ham
- 2 teaspoons cooking oil
- 2 eggs
- pepper

1. Spread butter on the bread slices.
2. Put two ham slices on each slice of bread.
3. Put the oil in a frying pan and heat it over medium heat. Crack the eggs into the frying pan when the oil is hot. Be careful not to break the yolks.
4. Cook the eggs until the whites are firm but the yolks are still runny. If you'd prefer yolks that aren't runny, cook the eggs until both the whites and yolks are firm. Add pepper to taste.
5. Use a spatula to carefully remove the fried eggs from the pan. Place them onto the ham. Serve the dish hot.

Frühstück
The German word for "breakfast" is *Frühstück* (FROO-shtook). Many German schools have a scheduled break for a second, smaller breakfast called *zweites Frühstück* (TSWAI-tess FROO-shtook).

Chilaquiles Origins

Chilaquiles (chee-la-KEE-lehs) can be traced back to the Indigenous Aztecs of Mexico. In the Nahuatl language spoken by the Aztecs, the word *chilaquiles* means "chilis and greens."

Mexican Chilaquiles Verdes

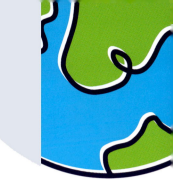

This dish originally became popular as a way to limit food waste by using up stale leftover tortillas. You can also make it with fresh tortilla chips.

Ingredients
(makes 4 servings)

- 1 avocado
- 3 tablespoons olive oil
- 16-ounce bottle of salsa verde
- 3 cups corn tortilla chips
- ½ teaspoon salt
- 4 tablespoons chopped fresh cilantro
- 4 eggs
- 3 green onions, chopped
- ⅓ cup crumbled Cotija cheese

1. Cut open the avocado and remove the pit. Then cut the flesh into slices while it is still in the peel. Use a spoon to scoop the slices into the small bowl. Set the bowl aside.

2. Heat 2 tablespoons of oil in a large frying pan over medium heat. Add the salsa verde. Turn up the heat to medium-high and let the salsa simmer for several minutes.

3. Remove the pan from the heat. Stir in the tortilla chips, salt, and 2 tablespoons of cilantro.

4. Heat the remaining oil in a small frying pan on medium-high heat. Crack the eggs into the pan, being careful not to break the yolks. Place the lid on the pan and cook the eggs for 5 minutes.

5. Use a spatula to scoop the chips and sauce onto the plates. Place an egg on each plate and top with the avocado, green onion, cheese, and remaining cilantro. Serve right away so the chips don't get too soggy.

Spanish Magdalenas

These lemon and olive oil muffins were traditionally baked for Spanish holidays. Today, they are a popular breakfast food found in many Spanish bakeries.

Ingredients
(makes 12 muffins)

- 3 eggs
- ½ cup sugar
- 1⅓ cup flour
- 2 teaspoons baking powder
- ½ teaspoon salt
- ½ cup olive oil
- 3 tablespoons milk
- zest of 1 lemon

1. Put the eggs and sugar in a mixing bowl. Beat with an electric mixer until the mixture turns light in color and has little bubbles.

2. In a separate bowl, whisk together the flour, baking powder, and salt. Add this to the egg mixture along with the oil, milk, and lemon zest. Mix until it is smooth. Cover the bowl with plastic wrap and put it in the refrigerator for 30 minutes.

3. Meanwhile, preheat the oven to 400 degrees Fahrenheit (200 degrees Celsius). Place baking cups in the muffin tin.

4. Take the mixture out of the fridge and scoop it into the baking cups. Each one should be about three-fourths full.

5. Bake the muffins for 15 minutes. Take them out of the oven and allow them to cool. Serve the muffins warm. Refrigerate the leftovers and enjoy them within three days.

A Sweet Story

One Spanish story claims that magdalenas (mag-dah-LAY-nahs) were named for a woman centuries ago who baked muffins and gave them to travelers arriving in Spain.

Jamaican Patois
English is Jamaica's official language. But many people also speak Jamaican Patois (Jah-MAY-can PAH-twah), a dialect with African, French, English, and other roots.

Jamaican Steamed Cabbage

Europeans likely introduced cabbage to Jamaica. Steamed cabbage is popular for its low cost and health benefits. Other veggies and meat are often added.

Ingredients
(makes 4 servings)

- 1 head of cabbage
- 3 tablespoons cooking oil
- 1 medium yellow onion, chopped
- 2 cloves of garlic, minced
- 2 small habanero peppers, diced
- 2 teaspoons thyme
- ½ tomato, chopped
- 1 large carrot, diced
- ½ bell pepper, diced
- 2½ teaspoons salt
- ½ teaspoon pepper

1. Cut the cabbage in half and remove the outer leaves. Cut the cabbage into wedges and then slice it into small shreds.

2. Heat the oil in a pot over medium-low heat. Add the onion, garlic, habanero peppers, and thyme. Sauté the mixture for two minutes, stirring occasionally. Add the tomato and sauté for another 2 minutes.

3. Add the cabbage and stir. Cover the pot and let the mixture steam for 10 minutes.

4. Stir in the carrots, bell pepper, salt, and pepper. Cover the pot to steam for 10 more minutes. Then serve the dish warm.

Zimbabwean Cornmeal Porridge

Porridge dishes in Zimbabwe date back to the ancient Shona people. Cornmeal became a staple in porridge after it was introduced to Zimbabwe in the 1500s.

Ingredients
(makes 1 serving)

- 4 tablespoons white cornmeal
- ½ cup milk
- 1 tablespoon sugar
- fresh fruit (optional)

1. Put the cornmeal and milk in a saucepan and stir until there are no lumps.
2. Heat the saucepan over medium heat. Stir the mixture until it thickens.
3. Once the mixture starts to boil, lower the heat and let it simmer for five minutes.
4. Stir in the sugar. Serve hot. If you'd like, add fresh fruit on top.

Sadza

Zimbabwean cornmeal porridge is often called *sadza* (SOD-zuh). Sadza can be made savory by subbing out the sugar for ¼ teaspoon salt. Savory sadza is usually eaten as a side dish.

Good Morning

Most people in Ireland speak English. But some people speak Irish too! "Good morning" in Irish is *maidin mhaith* (MAHD-zin wha).

Irish Full Breakfast

The full Irish breakfast was traditionally a meal for farmers. It gave them energy for long workdays. The meal is still common in Ireland today.

Ingredients
(makes 2 servings)

- 1 tablespoon cooking oil
- 1 tomato, cut into wedges
- 1 cup sliced mushrooms
- 6 precooked breakfast sausages
- 2 cups frozen hashbrowns
- salt to taste
- 8.3-ounce can pork and beans
- 4 eggs
- soda bread or sourdough bread

1. Heat half the cooking oil in a pan over medium heat. Add the tomato, mushrooms, and sausages. Cook covered for 5 to 8 minutes, stirring occasionally, until the tomatoes are soft and the mushrooms are browned.

2. Heat the hashbrowns in another frying pan according to the directions on the package. Sprinkle salt over the hashbrowns while they cook.

3. Heat the pork and beans according to the directions on the can. Use either a saucepan or a microwave-safe bowl.

4. Once the tomato, mushrooms, and sausages are cooked, set the ingredients aside on a plate. Add more cooking oil to the pan and heat it over medium-high heat. Crack the eggs into the pan, being careful not to break the yolks. Cook until the whites are firm and the yolks start to firm.

5. Serve everything together with a slice of soda bread or sourdough bread.

Moroccan Avocado Almond Smoothie Bowl

Avocado smoothies are popular in Morocco during the fasting month of Ramadan. The healthy, filling drinks help people stay full all day long!

Ingredients
(makes 2 servings)

- 1 large ripe avocado
- 1 cup almond milk (plain or vanilla)
- 1 teaspoon sugar or honey
- ¼ cup Greek yogurt
- toppings of your choice

1. Cut the avocado in half and remove the pit. Scoop out the flesh from the skin and put it in the blender.
2. Add the milk, sugar, and yogurt to the blender and blend until smooth.
3. Pour the smoothie into bowls and add toppings of your choice. In Morocco, some people add dried fruits such as figs and dates.

Say Avocado
Lavoka (lah-VOH-kah) means "avocado" in Moroccan Arabic, Morocco's official language.

Chinese Zucchini Pancakes

Rice is common in many Chinese dishes. But northern Chinese cooking is known for its flour-based dishes, such as pancakes, because rice does not grow well there.

Ingredients
(makes 8 to 10 pancakes)

- 1 zucchini
- 1 green onion, chopped
- ½ teaspoon salt
- ¼ teaspoon white pepper
- 2 eggs
- ½ teaspoon sesame oil
- ½ cup all-purpose flour
- 1 tablespoon cooking oil
- chili oil (optional)

Pancake Pronunciation
Zucchini pancakes are known as *Hú Tā Zi* (HOO tah zee) in Chinese.

1. Shred the zucchini onto a cutting board using the largest holes on the grater. Put the zucchini and green onion into a bowl.

2. Add the salt and white pepper to the bowl. Mix and let the mixture sit for 10 minutes.

3. Add the eggs and sesame oil to the bowl. Stir the mixture.

4. Add the flour to the bowl a little bit at a time, stirring between each addition, until the mixture is a thick batter.

5. Put the cooking oil in a frying pan. Heat the pan over medium-high heat.

6. Pour three spoonfuls of batter into the pan to make three pancakes. Spread the batter out evenly using the back of the spatula.

7. Cook the pancakes until the undersides are golden brown. Flip the pancakes with the spatula and cook until the other sides are golden brown too.

8. Repeat steps 6 and 7 until the batter is gone. Serve the pancakes plain or with chili oil.

Hawaiian Banana Bread

The Hawaiian island of Maui is famous for its sweet and moist banana bread. Local stands keep their recipes a secret. This recipe comes close to recreating the magic!

Ingredients
Makes 2 loaves (9 by 4 inches)

- 4 ripe bananas
- ½ cup plain Greek yogurt
- 2 eggs
- 2 teaspoons water
- 1 teaspoon vanilla extract
- 2 cups flour
- 1 cup sugar
- ¼ teaspoon salt
- 1 teaspoon baking powder
- 1 teaspoon baking soda
- ½ teaspoon cinnamon
- ¾ cup coconut oil
- ½ cup chopped pecans (optional)

1. Line two 9-by-4-inch (23-by-10-centimeter) loaf pans with parchment paper and preheat the oven to 350°F (177°C).

2. Peel the bananas. Use a fork to mash them in a mixing bowl. Stir in the yogurt, eggs, water, and vanilla extract.

3. Stir together the flour, sugar, salt, baking powder, baking soda, cinnamon, and coconut oil in another bowl. Stir in the banana mixture until no flour is visible. Then mix in the pecans, if using.

4. Pour the batter into the loaf pans. Bake the loaves for 50 minutes or until a toothpick inserted into the loaves comes out clean.

5. Take the loaves out of the oven and set the pans on a cooling rack for 10 minutes. Remove the bread from the pans and let it cool on the rack for another 10 minutes before slicing and serving.

Going Bananas

The Hawaiian word for "banana" is *mai'a* (MY-ah). Hawaii is home to several types of bananas not found in mainland stores. One is the apple banana, a small, sweet variety that's creamy and tangy.

Belarusian
Draniki Potato Pancakes

This potato pancake dish is often called the national dish of Belarus. The country eats the most potatoes per person of any nation in the world!

Ingredients
(makes 10 to 12 potato pancakes)

- 3 large Yukon Gold potatoes
- 1 small yellow onion
- 1 tablespoon lemon juice
- 1 egg
- 1 teaspoon salt
- 1 teaspoon pepper
- ¼ cup flour
- 4 tablespoons olive oil
- sour cream (optional)

Many Names

Many cultures have potato pancakes. They are called *draniki* (DRAH-neekee) in Belarus, *placki ziemniaczane* (PLOTZ-kee zhem-nyah-CHA-neh) in Poland, and *deruny* (DEH-roh-nee) in Ukraine.

1. Use a grater to shred the potatoes over a cutting board. Cut the onion into fourths and shred the onion. Put the potato and onion in a bowl with the lemon juice and mix.

2. Pour the potato and onion mixture into a colander. Use your hands to squeeze out the extra water over a sink.

3. Put the potato and onion mixture back in the bowl and stir in the egg, salt, and pepper. Add the flour and mix to make the batter.

4. Heat 1 tablespoon of olive oil in a frying pan over medium heat.

5. Scoop four separate spoonfuls of draniki batter into the pan. Cook the draniki until the bottoms are golden brown. Use a spatula and flip them over. Then cook the other sides until they are golden brown too.

6. Use the spatula to place the cooked draniki on a plate. Keep cooking draniki until you are out of batter. If the pan is dry, add more olive oil for cooking. Serve the draniki with sour cream if you'd like.

Indian
Rava Uttapam

These pancakes date thousands of years to the Tamil people of Southern India. They are often made with fermented rice and lentils but can be made with flour.

Ingredients
(makes 4 to 6 pieces)

- 2 cups semolina
- 1 cup Greek yogurt
- 2 teaspoons salt
- 1¾ cup water
- ½ teaspoon baking soda
- 3 tablespoons peanuts (optional)
- 1½ teaspoon cumin
- 2 cloves garlic
- 2 green chiles, chopped
- 1 tablespoon lemon juice
- 2½ cups chopped fresh cilantro or parsley
- ½ tomato, chopped
- ¼ onion, chopped
- 1 teaspoon chili powder
- olive oil

1. Make the batter. Mix the semolina, yogurt, 1 teaspoon salt, and 1 cup water in a mixing bowl. Mix in the baking soda. Place the towel over the bowl and set it aside for 20 minutes.

2. Make the chutney. Put the peanuts (if using), cumin, garlic, one green chili pepper, and the remaining salt in a blender. Add the lemon juice, ¼ cup water, and 2 cups herbs. Blend until smooth and set aside.

3. Make the topping. Combine the tomato, onion, chili powder, and remaining green chili and herbs in a small bowl.

4. Add the remaining water to the batter 1 tablespoon at a time until the batter is thick but can be poured. You may only need to use some of the water.

5. Heat 1 tablespoon of oil in a pan over medium-low heat. Scoop ⅓ cup batter into the pan. Use the back of the spoon to gently spread the batter into a circle.

6. Sprinkle some topping and ½ teaspoon oil on the batter. The oil will help the topping cook.

7. Cook each side of the uttapam for 2 to 3 minutes. Set the cooked uttapam aside and continue adding oil and cooking the rest of the uttapams. Serve them hot with chutney on the side.

Uttapam

Uttapam (UT-uh-pahm) is derived from the Tamil word *appam* (OP-uhm), which means "pancake." *Rava* (RAH-vuh) means "semolina," which is a granulated wheat.

A Beautiful Dish
Reina pepiada (RAY-nah peh-pee-AH-da) is an arepa (ah-RAY-pah) dish dating back to the 1950s. It features avocado and mayonnaise and was named for a Venezuelan beauty queen and celebrity.

Venezuelan Arepas

These stuffed cornmeal cakes date back to the Indigenous peoples of South America. They are considered a symbol of Venezuela's national identity.

Ingredients
(makes 4 to 6 arepas)

- 2 cups precooked white cornmeal
- 2½ cups warm water, plus 1 tablespoon
- 1 teaspoon salt
- 1 tablespoon cooking oil
- 2 tablespoons butter
- ½ white onion, chopped
- 2 cloves garlic, minced
- 1 ripe avocado
- 2 tablespoons mayonnaise
- 1 tablespoon chopped fresh cilantro

1. Preheat the oven to 350°F (177°C). Use your hands to mix the cornmeal, 2½ cups water, and salt in a mixing bowl. The mixture should look like bread dough.

2. Pour 1 tablespoon of water and the oil into a small bowl. Coat your hands in the liquid mixture so the dough won't stick to you. Roll a ball of dough the size of a small apple. Press it into a disk about ½ inch (1.3 cm) thick by transferring it from hand to hand. Once you have shaped your arepas, place them on a cutting board and cover them with a towel.

3. Heat the butter in a pan over medium-high heat. Cook the arepas for 4 to 5 minutes on each side.

4. Place the cooked arepas on a baking sheet. Bake them for 10 minutes.

5. Cook the onion and garlic over medium heat until they are soft and brown.

6. Cut the avocado in half and remove the pit. Scoop the avocado flesh into a bowl and mash it with a fork. Add the onion-and-garlic mixture and the mayonnaise to the avocado. Mix well.

7. Slice the arepas open. Fill each one with the avocado filling and a sprinkle of cilantro.

Read More

Hohn, Nadia L. *The Antiracist Kitchen: 21 Stories (and Recipes)*. Victoria, British Columbia: Orca Book Publishers, 2023.

Peterson, Tamara JM. *Eye-Opening Breakfasts in 15 Minutes or Less*. North Mankato, MN: Capstone, 2024.

Woollard, Rebecca. *The No-Cook Cookbook: More Than 50 Heat-Free Recipes for Young Chefs*. New York: DK Publishing, 2021.

Internet Sites

Breakfast Ideas from Around the World
superkidsnutrition.com/breakfast-around-the-world/

Ice for Breakfast: Turning River Ice into Hot Milk Tea in Mongolia
thekidshouldseethis.com/post/mongolia-river-ice-hot-milk-tea-breakfast

Is Breakfast Really the Most Important Meal of the Day?
wonderopolis.org/wonder/Is-Breakfast-Really-the-Most-Important-Meal-of-the-Day

About the Author

Chelsey Luciow is an artist and creator. She loves reading with kids and believes books are magical. Chelsey lives in Minneapolis with her wife, their son, and their dogs.